ELECTRICITY
For Beginners

TREVOR WRIGHTSON

Balboa Press books may be ordered through booksellers or by contacting:

Balboa Press
A Division of Hay House
1663 Liberty Drive
Bloomington, IN 47403
www.balboapress.com.au
AU TFN: 1 800 844 925 (Toll Free inside Australia)
AU Local: 0283 107 086 (+61 2 8310 7086 from outside Australia)

ISBN: 978-1-5043-2380-2 (sc)
ISBN: 978-1-5043-2381-9 (e)

Print information available on the last page.

Balboa Press rev. date: 03/02/2021

BALBOA.PRESS
A DIVISION OF HAY HOUSE

Electricity For Beginners

This book has been written for High School students, Electrical
Apprentices and those people interested in Electrical Theory.
It contains over fifty diagrams and is designed to give a very simple understanding of Electricity.
It will answer all those questions that you have been asking yourself if you have not come
into contact with the people who have this knowledge, or you are too embarrassed to ask.

Contents

Chapter One

WHAT IS ELECTRICITY?

INTRODUCTION

1.1   Welcome to the fascinating world of Electricity. Have you ever imagined living in a world without Electricity? No Electrical lighting or heating, no microwave oven or Electrical stove, no television, no refrigeration or computer. The list is endless, it just goes on and on, but have you ever stopped to think about, 'What is Electricity'? Where does it come from? How is it made?

I am hoping this book has all the answers for you.

Scientists tell us that Electricity is a flow of Electrons; Electrons leave an Atom and flow to the Atom in front of it. The Electron from that Atom leaves and flows to the Atom in front of it and so on. They travel at the same speed as light, 186,000 miles per second.

It has been said that a light switch in London when switched on, would light a globe in Sydney in one second.

After travelling around a circuit the Electrons return via a return cable back to the Atoms.

To understand this more fully we must understand more about the Atom.

Chapter Two

ATOMS

STRUCTURE OF AN ATOM

2.1   An Atom is so small that if a grain of sand was divided and a piece given to every person in the world, it would take each person twenty five years to count the number of Atoms in the piece of sand that they have been given.

The structure of the Atom is similar to the Solar System. At the centre is the Nucleus just like the Sun is the centre of our Solar System.

The Nucleus is composed of particles called Protons and Neutrons. Smaller particles called Electrons, orbit the Nucleus at different distances just the same as planets orbit the Sun.

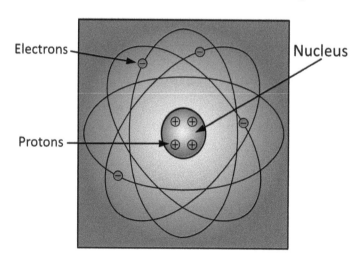

Fig 1 – Structure of an Atom

There is the same number of Electrons orbiting the Nucleus as there are Protons in the Nucleus of the Atom, it is said to be Electrically Neutral.

The Electrons are negatively charged whilst Protons in the Nucleus are positively charged.

When an Electron leaves an Atom there is not the same number of Electrons as Protons then the Atom is out of balance and said to be Positively Charged.

Electrons in the outer orbit of an Atom are called the Valence or Free Electron. This Electron being free may leave the orbit and flow to the outer orbit of the Atom next to it. The Electron in the outer orbit of this Atom then may leave and flow to the Atom next to it and so on. The reaction continues until the process is stopped.

Electrons in an Atom can be made to flow from an Atom, using three methods:

1. Chemically as in a battery.
2. Electromagnetically using a generator to generate Electricity
3. Static electricity made by nature.

When an Electron leaves the Atom, there is one less Electron than Protons. The Atom is said to be Positively Charged.

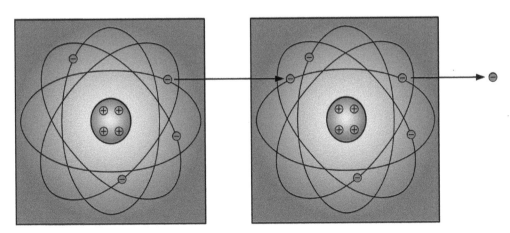

Fig 2 – Electricity is the Flow of Electrons

Chapter Three

TYPES OF ELECTRICITY

Electricity may be produced in three different ways:

3.1 ALTERNATING CURRENT (A.C.)

Alternating Current is produced in Power Stations by Alternators Electro Magnetically. The Electricity from the Alternators is transformed into high voltages and transmitted on overhead wires to different parts of the country. When it reaches its various locations it is transformed back to a suitable voltage and distributed to homes and factories. A.C. is the most common current used in our homes. It cannot be stored in batteries like Direct Current (D.C.).

3.2 DIRECT CURRENT (D.C.)

Direct Current is produced by a Generator and can be stored in a battery. It is most commonly used in motor vehicles, torches, toys, work tools and garden equipment. It is not suitable for household use.

3.3 STATIC ELECTRICITY

Electricity produced by nature is called Static Electricity. Static Electricity cannot be used and, in many cases is a source of annoyance.

When some objects are rubbed together, they will produce Static Electricity. The Electrons from one object will enter the other object 'charging it' with a very High Voltage.

You may have experienced Static Electricity whilst doing everyday chores such as walking across a carpet. The Electrons flow from the carpet charging your body with Electricity. When touching a metal frame or door handle it discharges, the Electrons are released from your body in the form of a very high Voltage which results in you receiving an Electric shock. The Electrons then flow back to the carpet when they are released from your body.

When you get out of a car whilst wearing rubber soled shoes, your body is charged with millions of Electrons. As soon as you touch the door to close it the Electrons flow from your body back to the car, causing you to receive an Electric shock. Although the Voltage is in the order of thousands of Volts, the current is negligible.

Fig 3 – Static Electric Shock

If you do not touch the car the Electrons will slowly dissipate through your shoes back into the ground and eventually back into the car.

During the early part of this century petrol tankers which were transporting petrol, were blown up due to static Electricity causing a spark which ignited the petrol.

The petrol, sloshing around in the tank was charged by the Electrons from the road. These Electrons built up a very high and dangerous voltage which caused an ark similar to lightning and ignited the petrol. Mechanics corrected the fault by bolting a chain to the frame of the truck and dangling onto the road, thus, allowing the Electrons to disperse back to the roadway.

A similar effect is during a rainstorm, clouds moving in the sky 'rip' the Electrons from the ground, trees and buildings. The result is the clouds are charged with 'Billions' of volts until the voltage is so high that it can't restrain it any longer, resulting in severe lightening.

Another effect occurs, when cars travelling across a bridge are charged with static Electricity and when the driver payed the toll at the end, both the driver and toll collector receive a severe Electric shock.

As a result, tolls were paid before entering the bridge or a piece of wire was fixed to the road which protruded high enough so as the vehicle would strike it and release the static charge that is contained in the vehicle. People sitting inside the car could actually hear the 'zap' of the discharge which occurred several meters in front of the toll cubicle when it hits the wire.

Scientists are trying to devise a way of harnessing static electricity from storms otherwise it is a source of annoyance which in many cases has resulted in the death of many people.

Chapter Four

ELECTRICAL TERMS AND DEFINITIONS

CONDUCTORS

4.1   Conductors are substances which allow Electrical current to readily flow through them. They may be solid, liquid or gaseous.

All metals are conductors; some metals are better conductors than others. The best three conductors of Electricity are the metals silver, copper and gold in that order.

Gold and silver cannot seriously be considered as conductors because of their cost.

Copper is the most common conductor.

Silver is the best conductor of Electricity and has been given the relative conductivity of 100%. All other conductors are based relative to it.

Copper is the next best conductor with one valence Electron in its outer orbit and has a relative conductivity of 96%, whilst gold with one valence Electron is 73% ; aluminium has three valence Electrons, with a relative conductivity of 59%.

Aluminium conductors are not as good a conductor as copper, but are used in Transmission lines over vast distances. They are used because it is lighter and cheaper than copper.

Most conductors are covered with insulation to prevent them touching other conductors, and framework of containers or other component parts, which would cause 'short circuit' resulting in excessive current being drawn and 'blowing' a fuse or tripping a circuit breaker.

Most conductors are cables that are used for high Voltage have a higher grade insulation than low Voltage cables. There are many types of cables made, Single stranded cables, Multi-stranded cables. Other cables have many cores of insulated cables and covered with an outer insulating sheath.

Single strand cables are inclined to break with movement and should be installed in situations where they will not be disturbed. Single strand cables may be used in walls and ceilings of buildings where they are not moved.

Multi stranded cables are used where there is excessive movement of cables, as in cars and moving vehicles or electrical appliances with attached flexible cables, such as Electric appliances, irons, toasters and extension leads etc. Multi stranded cables are expensive to manufacture.

Cables are measured by the 'cross sectional area' of the conductors. i.e. 1.0mm sq., 1.5mm sq., 2.5mm sq., 4.0mm sq., 16mm sq. etc. The two most common cables used would be 1.5mm sq. used for wiring lights and 2.5mm sq. used for wiring power points, stoves and hot water systems.

If you increase the current in a circuit, a larger size conductor must also be used to carry the additional current. It is important that you select the correct size cable for the job.

Containers of cables have a label on the side of the drum indicating the Insulation size and the voltage.

INSULATORS

4.2   If you were to touch an Electrical conductor, you would receive an Electrical shock. To prevent you from receiving an Electrical shock, conductors are covered with insulation.

Insulation or Insulators are substances which resist the displacement of its Electrons. They are usually manufactured, or are of a non-metallic substance such as rubber, Polyvinyl and chloride (plastic). In the early times most cables were insulated with rubber, but since the nineteen fifties rubber has been replaced with Plastic Sheathing.

If higher voltage cables are used higher grade insulation is required than low Voltage cables.

CIRCUITS

4.3   A Circuit is when an applied voltage either A.C. or D.C. (Active if it is A.C. or Positive if it is D.C.), current will flow through an appliance and return back to a Neutral A.C. or Negative D.C. The circuit is said to be complete.

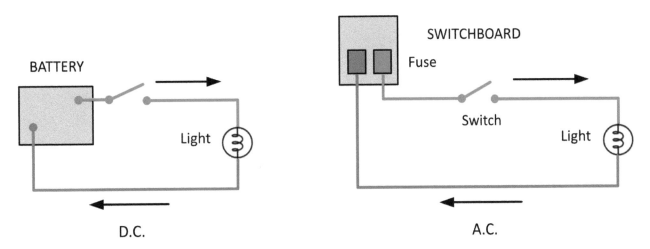

Fig 4 – Typical Circuits

Confusion can occur when the main supply to D.C. is called Positive and Negative and the main supply to A.C. is called Active and Neutral. Also, the main supply is referred to as Main Supply, Applied Voltage and Electro Motive Force (EMF) they all mean the same thing 'Main Supply'.

When a source of supply is applied to an Electrical Circuit and the circuit is complete there is a flow of Electrons, this motion is known as Electrical Current and is measured in Amperes (Amps) and has a symbol of 'I'.

Electrical current flowing in a circuit can be likened to water flowing in a pipe. If a pipe is full of water and the valve or tap is turned off, there is no flow of water and there will be no current flow in the water, a fish could swim in either direction in the water. If the valve is turned on then the water will flow and the water has current. 'Heh!... What happened to the little fish?'

Similarly, in an Electrical Circuit, if a source of supply is applied to a switch and the switch is turned OFF there is no flow of Electrical Current. If the switch is turned ON, the circuit is complete then there is a flow of current.

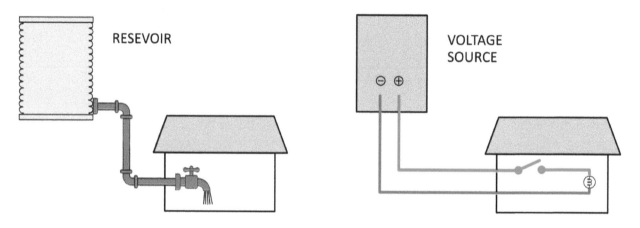

Fig 5 – Current Flowing in a Circuit

The current will increase or decrease according to the amount of load in the circuit. The load can be referred to as any Electrical appliance in an Electrical Circuit. If the load is increased then the current will increase, if the load is decreased then the current will decrease.

VOLTAGE

4.4 Voltage is the unit of pressure of Electricity to force the current to flow. It is termed 'Applied Voltage' and is measured in Volts and has a symbol of 'E' or 'V'. The greater the applied Voltage, then the greater the current will flow.

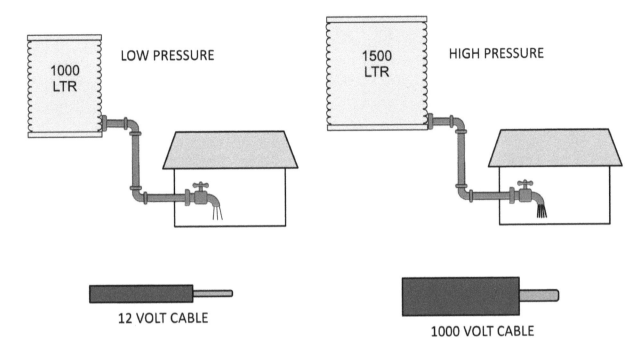

Fig 6 – The Higher the Voltage the Greater the Insulation

If the water pressure in a pipe increased sufficiently then the pipe would split. Similarly in an Electrical circuit, if you increase the voltage on a cable it would puncture the cable. A cable with higher insulation should be used.

VOLTAGE DROP

4.5   Electricity is transmitted at three hundred and thirty thousand volts to overcome Voltage drop. Voltage in a cable will drop over a distance, for example, if a voltage of five thousand volts is transmitted to Sydney and there is a voltage drop of one hundred volts then the voltage received in Sydney is four thousand nine hundred volts. To overcome the voltage drop, the voltage is transformed to three hundred and thirty thousand volts. The voltage drop will remain one hundred volts and when the voltage is transformed back down to household use, the voltage drop is negligible.

RESISTANCE

4.6   Resistance is a very important function in an Electrical Circuit.

A resistor is a conductor which offers resistance to the flow of current and is measured in Ohms. It has the symbol 'Oh mega' Ω

The most important feature of a resistor is any material which resists Electricity will heat up. Insulators such as rubber, plastic, paper and dry wood have so much resistance they prevent a flow of electricity to pass through them.

Resistors made of Carbon have coloured bands around them to indicate their resistance value and are used in Electronic equipment. Resistors made of wire are used in stoves and elements in light globes etc.

Any loose connection in an Electrical Circuit will resist the flow of current and is considered high resistive joint and will heat up and may cause a fire.

OHMS LAW

4.7   There is a direct relationship between Voltage, Current and Resistance. If a voltage of one Volt is applied to a circuit which has a resistance of one Ohm, a Current of one Amp will flow. This principal is known as 'Ohms law' and is expressed as 'E' or 'V' = 'I' x 'R'.

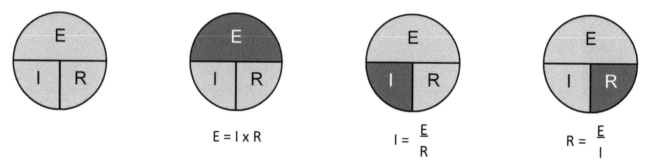

Fig 7 – Ohms Allows you to Calculate Voltage Current and Resistance in a Circuit

WATTS

4.8   The amount of Electricity consumed in a circuit is expressed as power and is measured in Watts.

A Watt is the amount of energy of Electricity used or consumed in one second, by a current of one Ampere under a pressure of one Volt.

Many Electrical appliances are rated in Watts, stoves, electric motors and in particular, light globes.

One thousand Watts equals one Kilowatt.

Seven hundred and forty six Watts is equal to one horsepower.

Chapter Five

MAGNETS

TYPES OF MAGNETS

5.1   One component, that has the greatest influence on Electricity, is a Magnet.
    A. There are two main types of magnets:
    1. Bar Magnets
    2. Electromagnets.

We have all at one stage played with Magnets, but have you realised all the different features of a magnet.

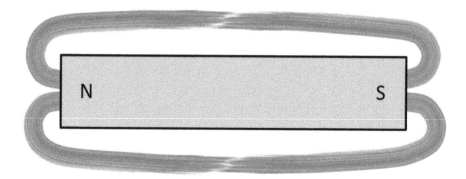

Fig 8 – Bar Magnet

BAR MAGNET

5.2   The features of a Bar Magnet are:

A. They have the ability to attract.
B. They have a Magnetic field commonly known as the 'flux'
C. They have a North and South Pole.
D. If two magnets are held close to each other with the same poles they will repel each other, 'Unlike' poles will attract each other.

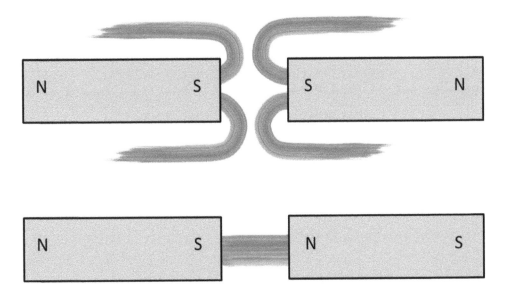

Fig 9 – Like Poles Repel each other. Unlike Poles Attract each other

E. Magnets are made in either horseshoe shape or flat bar shape.
F. If a Bar Magnet is suspended in the middle on a piece of string, the North Pole will point to the Earth's Magnetic pole (This is the function of a compass).
G. A Magnet will lose its Magnetic Field if it is struck with a hammer or a hard object.
H. Hard steel will remain magnetised.
I. Soft iron loses its magnetism almost immediately after it has been magnetised. They are not used as permanent Magnets.
J. The ability for a piece of steel to retain a magnetic field is known as 'Permeability'.
K. The ability for a piece of steel to retain a magnetic field is 'Retentivity'.
L. If a magnet is required to be stored, a piece of steel known as a 'Keeper' should be placed across the poles, this will allow it to retain its magnetism.

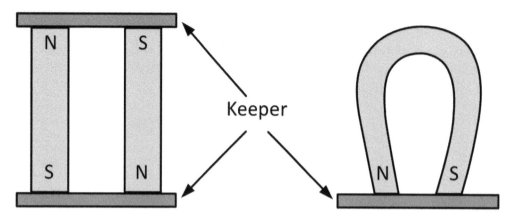

Fig 10 – To keep the Magnetism in a Magnet they require a Keeper

ELECTROMAGNETS

5.3   When insulated copper wire is wound around a piece of iron or steel and an Electrical voltage is applied, it will become magnetised.

The features of an Electromagnet are:

- A. If the Voltage is increased in an Electromagnet, the Magnetic field will increase.
- B. If the Voltage is decreased, then the Magnetic Field will decrease.
- C. If the number of turns of insulated wire is increased, the Magnetic Field will Increase.
- D. If the number of turns of insulated wire is reduced, then the Magnetic Field will reduce.
- E. If the Voltage is reversed then the poles will reverse.

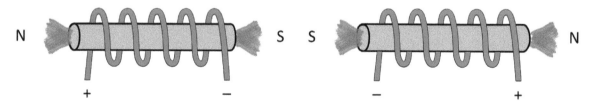

Fig 11 – If the Voltage is reversed the Poles will reverse.

F.   If a piece of insulated wire is wound around a piece of hard steel it will remain permanently magnetised when the Voltage is switched off.

G.   If a piece of insulated wire is wound around a piece of soft iron and a Voltage is applied, it will become magnetised and remain magnetised until the Voltage is switched off.

H.   A small amount of magnetism which is known as 'Residual Magnetism' will remain in soft iron after it is switched off.

EDDY CURRENTS

5.4   When a coil is wound on a solid block of iron as well as a Magnetic Field cutting the Winding, the Magnetic Field also cuts the iron core inducing it with A.C. This is known as 'Eddy Currents'. To prevent this happening the iron core is replaced with laminations.

Laminations are made from sheets of soft iron 1mm thick. They are cut to shape and placed into position and are insulated from each other with either tissue paper or allowing each sheet to lightly rust, this prevents Eddy Currents forming. Each sheet of laminate is induced with a voltage. Because they are insulated from each other, the total voltage in the block is negligible.

Electrical Motors, Relays, Transformers and Contactors etc. are made of Laminations to prevent Eddy Currents.

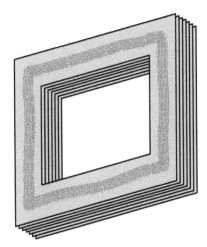

Fig 12 – The Iron Block is changed to laminations 1 mm thick

Chapter Six

A.C. INDUCTION

GENERATION

6.1   An extremely important feature in Electrical Theory is when a Conductor or a piece of insulated wire is moving through a Magnetic Field, and then an EMF or Voltage is induced in the conductor.

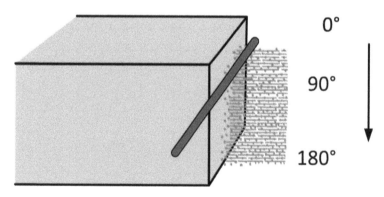

Fig 13 – A Conductor moving through a Magnetic Field

As the conductor begins to pass through the Magnetic Field, the Voltage will begin to rise. It will continue to rise until it reaches the centre of the field, where maximum Voltage is reached. As it descends from the field, the Voltage will decrease until it passes out of the field where it returns to zero.

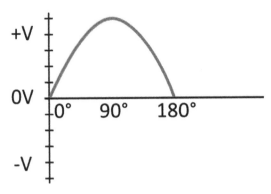

Fig 14 – A Half of a Cycle produced moving through a field of a Magnet

If two Magnets are secured opposite each other, with their 'Unlike Poles' trying to attract each other, and a conductor is placed in the Magnetic Field and forced to revolve three hundred and sixty degrees around and close to the poles, a full cycle of Alternating Current is generated.

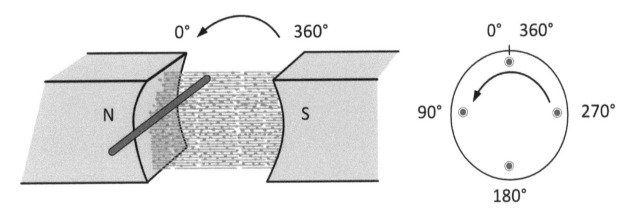

Fig 15 – A Conductor moving through 360 degrees of Two Magnetic poles

As the Conductor passes through the field of one pole it will produce a half cycle of Alternating Current, which is Positive. Then as it passes through the Magnetic Field of the opposite pole it is induced with the Negative part of the cycle.

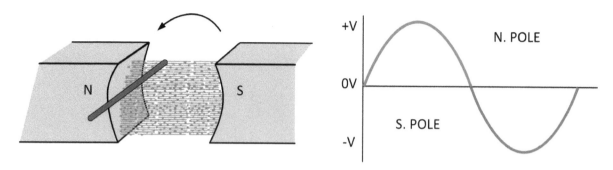

Fig 16 – A full A.C. Cycle produced passing through 360 degrees

One complete cycle is one revolution of three hundred and sixty degrees.

If the Conductor is forced to continually revolve then the Alternating Current produced would continue until it is stopped.

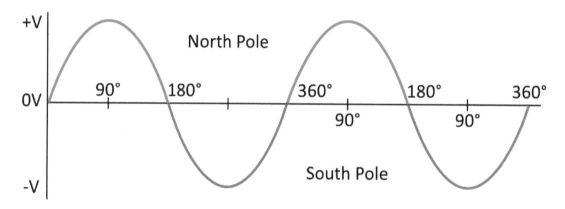

Fig 17 – A Conductor revolving Non Stop through Magnetic Fields

It can be said that the Voltage flowing in an Alternating Circuit is rising and falling in a Conductor and is proportional to the speed it travels through 360 degrees. This is known as the Frequency and is measured in Cycles or Hertz per Second.

Millions of Electrons flow in a Conductor in one second. They travel in one direction for one half of a cycle. In the second half of the cycle they travel in the opposite direction.

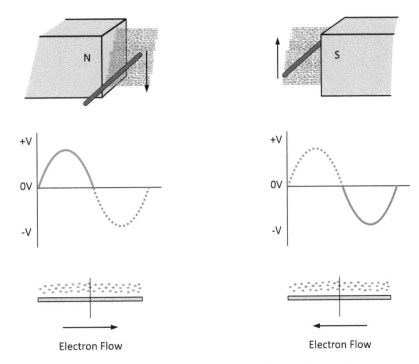

Fig 18 – Electrons flow in One Direction for Half a Cycle and in the Reverse Direction for the Second Half of The Cycle

CONVENTIONAL CURRENT

6.2   In a Direct Current Circuit the Electrons flow from Negative to Positive.

In an Alternating Current Circuit, the Electrons flow in one direction for the first half of a cycle, then in the opposite direction for the second half of the cycle.

Confusing isn't it?

Before the Electron Theory came along, Current was thought to travel from Positive to Negative. It was decided to leave it as it was and is now known as Conventional Current. So as we know it, Current flows from Positive to Negative.

Chapter Seven

ALTERNATOR

A.C. GENERATION

7.1   An Alternator generates Alternating Current.

If a loop of insulated wire is suspended on a shaft, which has a bearing on each end and is placed in a field (between two opposite poles) and is forced to revolve, then an EMF or Voltage is induced in the loop.

If two wheels are attached and insulated from the shaft and one end of the loop is soldered to each wheel, then a Voltage of A.C. may be obtained from the two wheels. The two wheels are referred to as 'Slip Rings' and are made from brass.

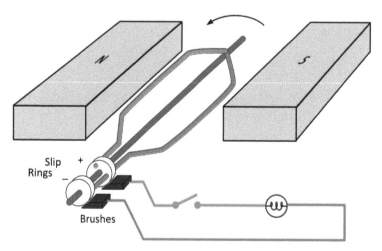

Fig 19 – A Single Phase Alternator and Circuit

A method of 'picking up' the Voltage from Slip Rings, is with carbon blocks referred to as 'Brushes'. The Brushes make contact with the Slip Rings under spring tension and are held in a box known as Brush Boxes.

Carbon is used because it is a good Conductor and is subject to very little wear of the Slip Rings and also itself.

If a switch is placed in the active wire and closed, it will operate a Simple Circuit.

If the Magnetic Field is Increased or Decreased, the output Voltage would Increase or Decrease.

If the loop was forced around slowly, then a light would light on and off slowly. If the loop is forced around fast, the light would light on and off fast.

Alternators in a Power Station revolve at three thousand Revolutions per minute and generate a Frequency of 50 cycles per second. In actual fact, your lights at home are turning on and off at fifty times per second, which of course is too fast for you to see and appear to be on all the time.

Alternators are forced to revolve by several different methods:

- Diesel Driven Motors
- Steam/Coal Driven Turbines
- Hydro Driven Turbines
- Nuclear Powered
- Wind Powered
- Ocean Powered

Diesel Driven Alternators are installed in isolated areas. It is cheaper to install diesel Alternators than to install Transmission lines over a vast distance.

Steam/Coal Driven Alternators are used in countries where there are huge deposits of coal or Uranium, such as Australia. The coal or Uranium is used to heat water, which produces steam. The steam turns a turbine which is attached to the rotor of an alternator which revolves and produces

Electricity. Coal fired Steam Driven Turbines produce a huge amount of CO2 which is causing Global Warming.

Hydro Driven Alternators produce the cheapest form of Electricity and don't produce any pollution. They are driven by water, which is stored in large dams above the Alternators and at night when power is not required, they run the Alternators as a motor and pump the water back up into the dams. Hydro driven Power Stations are built where heavy rain or heavy snow falls.

Nuclear Power Stations are built in Countries that have no coal Reserves for Coal Fired Power Stations or Hydro Schemes. They are cheaper to run than Coal Fired Power Stations, but they have the disadvantage of a meltdown, exposing Nuclear Radiation. Two Power Stations one in Russia and one in Japan have had a Nuclear Melt Down, causing catastrophic problems.

Chapter Eight

THREE PHASE ALTERNATORS

THREE PHASE

8.1 The three phases (conductors) are placed one hundred and twenty degrees apart and are joined at one end called the Star Point.

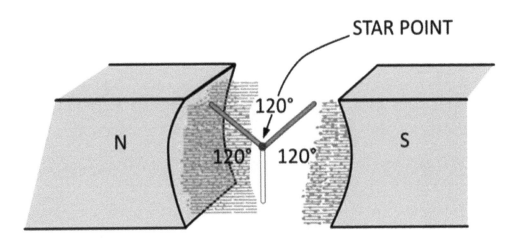

Fig 20 – Three Phases 120 degrees apart passing through a Magnetic Field

The RED phase passes through a Magnetic Field first, followed by the WHITE Phase, one hundred and twenty degrees later and then the BLUE a further one hundred and twenty degrees later.

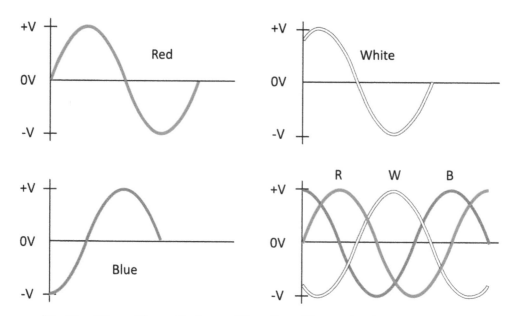

Fig 21 – Three Phase Cycles as They Pass Through a Magnetic Field

The RED Phase passes past a Magnetic Pole, followed one hundred and twenty degrees later by the WHITE or YELLOW Phase and then followed one hundred and twenty degrees later by the BLUE phase.

The following drawing shows the RED phase passing a given point firs, followed by the WHITE/YELLOW and then the BLUE.

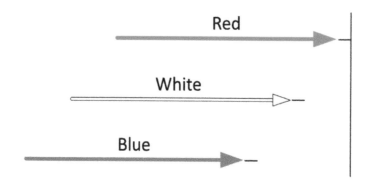

Fig 22 – Each Phase arrives at a given Point at a Different Time

As modern day Alternators progressed and increased in output and size, the brushes which picked up the output in the original Alternators became an enormous problem.

To overcome this problem the Three Phase Windings are placed in the Stator (casing).

The rotor was converted to two poles that has one hundred and twenty Volts D.C. supply to magnetise them. The Rotor rotated inside the Stator, the Magnetic Field cutting the Three Phase Winding at a speed of 3,000 rpm, producing a frequency of 50 cycles. The Star Point of the Alternator Winding is earthed. The output from the machine is transformed and fed into the grid system to help meet the system demands.

The advantages of a Three Phase Alternator over a Single Phase Alternator are:

1. The load from a Three Phase Alternator is spread over three Phases instead of one single Phase
2. The maximum size of a Single Phase motor is 5 horsepower. Three Phase motors can be made up to several hundred horsepower.
3. Three Phase Motors are more efficient and run a lot smoother and don't require a starting device as single phase motors do.

Note: the load is distributed evenly in each phase of a three phase alternator and it is termed 'Balanced Load'.

The following drawing shows a Three Phase Alternator, with a 120 volt D.C. Rotator Field, cutting the Three Phase Stator Winding.

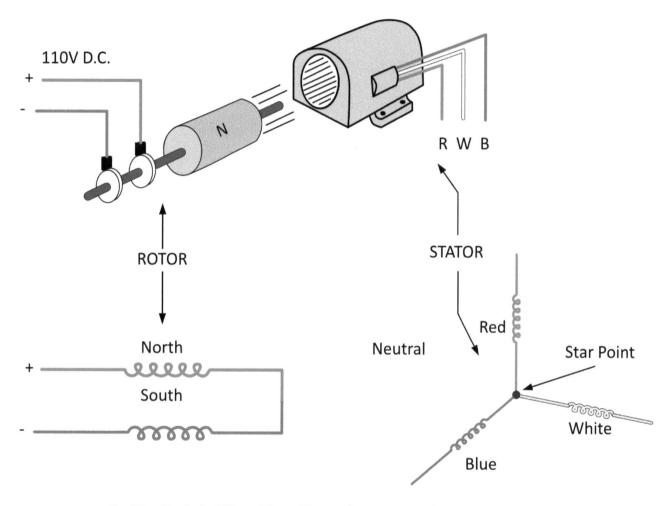

Fig 23 – Exploded View. Three Phase Alternator with Rotor and Stator

The following drawing shows a Three Phase Alternator with current flowing through a Three Phased Balanced Load and returning via the Neutral to the Star Point.

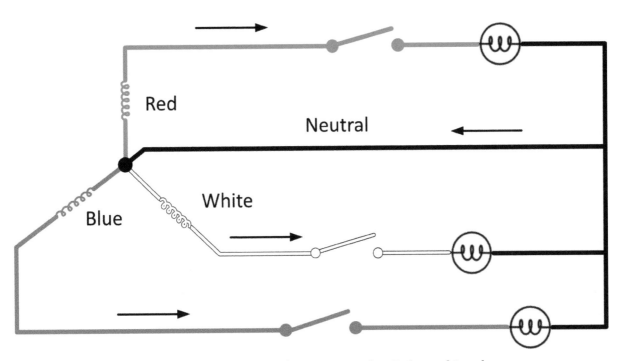

Fig 24 – Three Phase Alternator with a Balanced Load

Chapter Nine

TRANSFORMERS

TRANSFORMER REACTION

9.1   Quite often we require a Voltage, which is different to the Supply Voltage.

A Transformer as the name implies, transforms one Voltage to the Voltage that is required.

Transformers are used frequently in our homes. Electronic equipment such as television, radios, video's and dish washes etc., require Transformers.

When insulated copper wire is wound around a piece of soft iron and an Electrical Voltage is applied, the iron will become magnetised.

If A.C. which is pulsating is applied to the coil then the Magnetic Field will pulsate. If D.C. is applied to the coil the Magnetic Field will be stable.

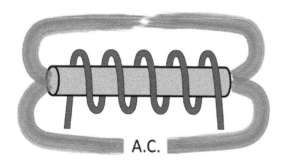

A.C.

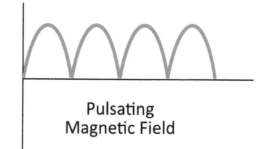

Pulsating
Magnetic Field

Fig 25 – When A.C. is applied to an Electromagnet then the Field will pulsate

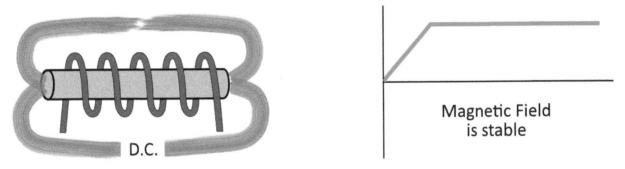

Fig 26 – When D.C. is applied to an Electromagnet then the field will remain stable

When a conductor is passed through a magnetic field of a bar magnet, then an A.C. voltage is induced in the conductor.

When A.C. is applied to a coil wound around a piece of soft iron then the magnetic field will pulsate. If a conductor or a coil is placed in the pulsating magnetic field then the pulsating field will cut the conductor and a voltage will be induced in the conductor.

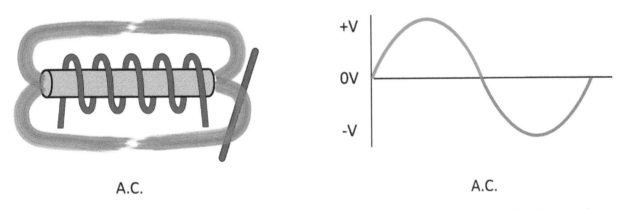

Fig 27 – When a Conductor is passed through a Magnetic Field then A.C. is induced in the conductor

If a square hole is cut in a block of iron and a coil is wound around one side of it, and an A.C. Voltage applied, then a pulsating Magnetic Field is induced into the block.

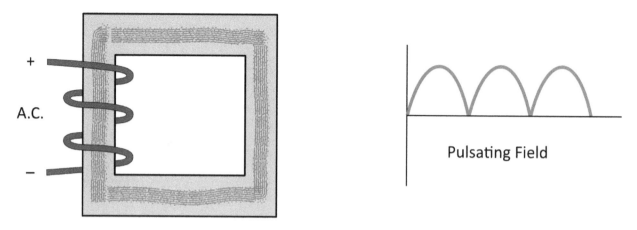

Fig 28 – When A.C. is applied to the Coil the Block is magnetised with a Pulsating Field

When a second coil is wound around the block opposite the Primary coil, the Magnetic Field will cut the second coil inducing a Voltage in it. The coils are known as the Primary and Secondary Windings of a Transformer.

Instead of moving the conductor through the pulsating field as in an Alternator, the field is moving through the conductor. This action is known as Transformer Reaction.

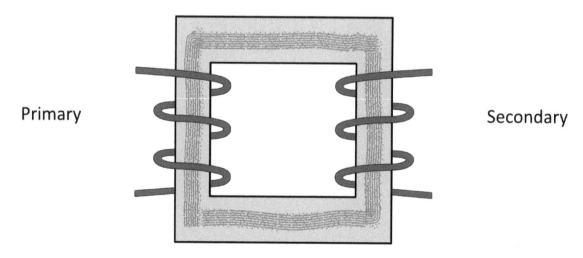

Fig 29 – Transformer with a Primary and Secondary Winding

Transformers can either step up or step down voltages. The voltage and output are dependent on the size of the wire and the number of turns of the Windings.

A transformer is similar to an Alternator. The rotating field of an Alternator cuts the Conductors in the Stator Windings inducing a Voltage. With a Transformer the pulsating Magnetic Field cuts the Secondary Winding and inducing a Secondary Voltage.

The physical size of a Transformer varies according to the load requirements. Small Transformers as big as a five cent piece are used in electronic equipment, whilst transformers are as big as a truck, are used in heavy industry.

Chapter Ten

DIRECT CURRENT (D.C.)

10.1 D.C. is produced in Two Ways:

    A. Electro Magnetically using a Generator
    B. Stored in a Battery

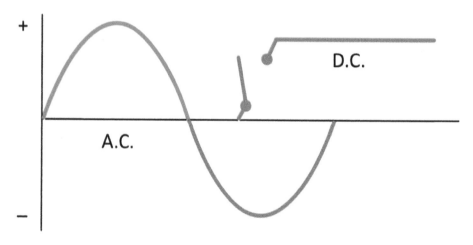

Fig 30 – A.C. is a Cycle and D.C. is a Straight Line

A.C. voltage pulsates, a D.C. voltage is stable.

ADVANTAGES OF D.C.

10.2

    A. Direct Current can be stored in a Battery and is used in portable equipment, such as hand tools, garden equipment, torches and toys.

B. Lithium batteries have an extremely high reliable performance, and can be recharged. They are used in vital equipment, such as pacemakers, Medical and Military equipment.
C. The voltage from a D.C. Battery is very stable unlike pulsating A.C. and is used in equipment where a stable voltage is required.

DISADVANTAGES OF D.C.

10.3

A. D.C. Generators require a Commutator, which are very complex and expensive to make.
B. D.C. is not transformed very often as it is a very complicated process.

D.C. GENERATOR

10.4   A D.C. Generator is similar to an A.C. Alternator. The fields of a D.C. Generator are placed in the outer casing. The Rotor is an Armature which houses the Windings and rotates, cutting the field of the outer casing. The generated Voltage is transferred to a Commutator, which is located on the end of the shaft of the Armature. The Voltage picked up from the Commutator by Carbon Brushes and then distributed into the system.

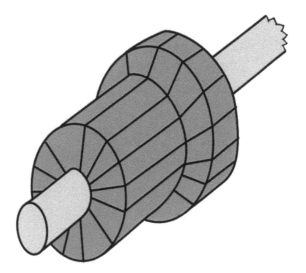

Fig 31 – D.C. Commutator

Commutators are made of copper segments, which are insulated from each other and placed side by side in a cylindrical shape and fitted to the end of the Armature. Each end of the Winding is soldered to a segment of the Commutator.

A Commutator converts A.C. to D.C. When each Winding of the Armature is in the centre of a pole, the Voltage travels to the end of the Winding, soldered to a segment. The current is then picked up from the Commutator by a brush and distributed into the system.

The segments of a Commutator have a gap for insulation. Each time the brushes pass over a gap, there is a small time delay between each segment which causes a ripple in the Voltage.

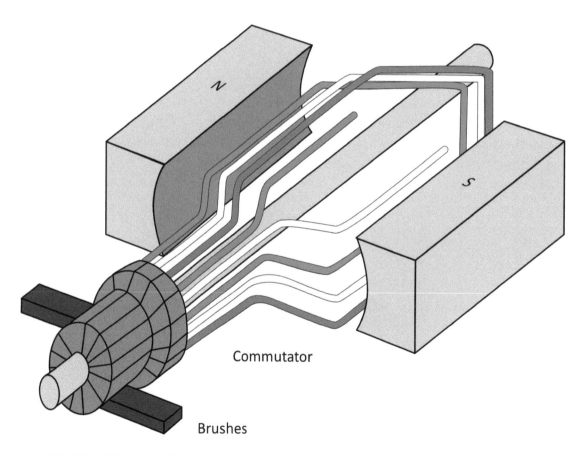

Commutator

Brushes

Fig 32 – The ends of the Windings are attached to segments of a Commutator

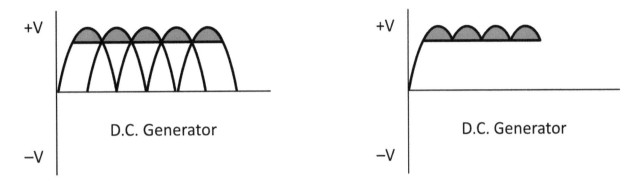

Fig 33 – The D.C. generated by a Generator has a ripple

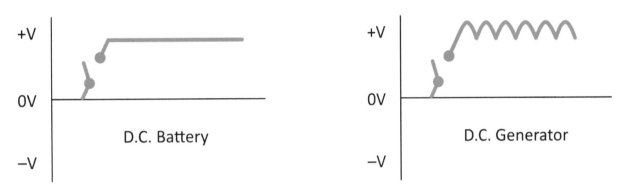

Fig 34 – D.C. Voltage from a Battery can be expressed as a Straight Line.
D.C. generated by a Generator has a ripple

DRY CELL BATTERIES

10.5   There are eight types of Dry Cell Batteries. Four canister type, (of which two are rechargeable) and four button type, which are small, flat and round in shape which fit in watches, hearing aids, cameras, calculators and instruments etc. Lithium and Ni Cad Batteries are the only Dry Cell Batteries that can be recharged.

Note: Dry Cell Carbon Zinc Batteries cannot be recharged and when they are discharged have to be discarded.

LITHIUM BATTERIES

Lithium Batteries have a huge advantage over other Batteries, their cost is quite modest. Because of their huge storage capacity they are used for storing Solar Power in houses and used in Solar Farms for the National Grid System. Operating temperatures have little effect on their operating characteristics and they can be used for many years.

NI CAD BATTERIES

Ni Cad Batteries are rechargeable and may be stored for long periods, either in charged or discharged state. If they are stored in a charged state they will discharge at approximately two percent per day and should be recharged every two months.

It is very important to remember that Ni Cad batteries have a peculiar phenomenon and can form a memory.

Ni Cad Batteries are used in Spaceships as they can be recharged with Solar Cells from the sun and last up to ten years.

Carbon Zinc Batteries

Carbon Zinc Batteries are the most used battery. It is the least expensive battery made and is often referred to as the work horse. It is mostly used in torches toys and radios. When it is flat it is discarded.

The Batteries are made in a container made from Zinc, which is the Negative. In the centre of the can is a Carbon Rod, which is the Positive. Between the Rod and the canister is a porous type material, which is saturated with the Electrolyte. Some Dry Cells use a Liquid Electrolyte whilst the majority use a paste, to prevent spillage.

Fig 35 – A Typical Carbon Zinc Dry Cell Battery

WET CELL BATTERY

10.6   Wet Cells or Acid Batteries can be recharged when they are flat. Wet Acid Batteries are used in motor vehicles and have an enormous workload. A motor car's starter motor has to turn the engine of a motor vehicle to start the car. The starter motor draws a hefty fifty five amps to start a motor vehicle. The Battery is then recharged from a D.C. Generator fitted to the car's engine.

Lead Acid Batteries consists of a series of lead plates placed side by side. The lead plates, one positive and one negative are kept uniformly apart by insulated material of either wooden sheets or glass rods.

The lead plates are installed in a battery case, which is made from plastic or hardened rubber then they are covered in a solution of diluted sulphuric acid and distilled water. When the plates of the Battery are charged, the specific gravity of the acid alters.

The amount of charge in a battery may be obtained by measuring the specific gravity using a hydrometer. The Battery is fully charged when the specific gravity (SG) reading of the hydrometer is 1.280 or above. If the SG falls to around 1.100 then the battery is flat.

Fig 36 – Wet Cell Battery

During the course of use, a battery will lose some of the water through evaporation causing the acid level to drop below the plates. The level should be checked frequently and topped up to one centimetre above the plates with distilled water.

Note. Batteries can become heated and some of the water will evaporate and must be topped up. DO NOT top up with acid as it is only the water that evaporates and not the acid. Highly inflammable hydrogen gas is given off from batteries naked flames must be kept away from lead acid batteries, and particularly when they are being recharged and they are gassing and bubbling.

If a lead acid battery is required to be stored for any period of time, then it should be fully charged, the acid tipped out and then placed into storage. When it is required for use again, the acid may be replaced, given a small charge and placed into service.

Lead Acid Batteries are preferred over Alkaline Batteries because of the high initial manufacturing cost of alkaline cells.

ALKALINE BATTERIES

10.7   There are two types of Alkaline Batteries:
- Nickel Iron
- Nickel Cadmium

The Electrolyte (Acid) used in both the Nickel Iron and Nickel Cadmium is Potassium Hydroxide and is fully charged when the specific gravity reading is about 1.19.

Alkaline Batteries are mainly used for Industrial purposes.

SUMMARY

10.8
- A   A.C. is used in homes and industry, it is simpler to produce.
- B   A.C. can be transformed.
- C.   D.C. is generated using a D.C. Generator and can be stored in a Battery.
- D.   As D.C. is stable it is the preferred Voltage in vital equipment, as A.C. pulsates.
- E.   Voltage from a Battery is very stable. Voltage from a Generator has a slight ripple.

Chapter Eleven

SERIES AND PARALLEL CIRCUITS

ELECTRICAL CIRCUITS AND APPARATUS

11.1   Electrical circuits and apparatus may be connected in either Parallel or Series.

PARALLEL CIRCUITS

11.2   Most circuits and apparatus are connected in parallel, as it has the same voltage applied to each component in the circuit.

When apparatus containing resistance is connected in Series, the voltage drops each time it passes through a component.

Switches have no resistance and are connected in Series with an apparatus.

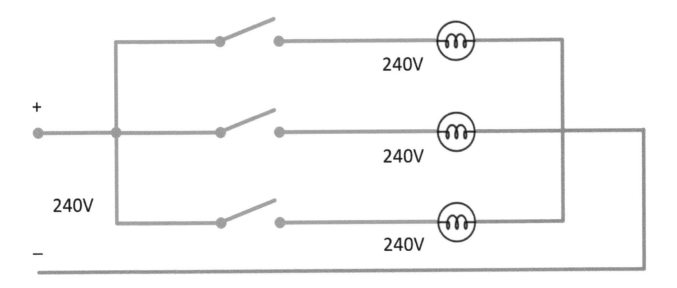

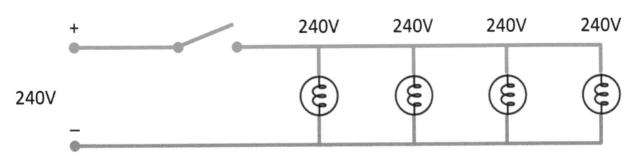

Fig 37 – Lights Connected in Parallel

It can be seen that each light has 240 volts the same voltage to each globe. If one globe blows it has no effect on the other globes.

SERIES CIRCUITS

11.3   When lights are connected in Series, the Voltage drops as it passes through each globe. The more globes you place in series the greater the Voltage will drop and the lights will become weaker.

Lights are not connected in Series very often. Christmas tree lights are connected in Series. They have the disadvantage that, if one globe blows then all the lights go out. It is very hard to find which globe is blown, as each globe has to be checked individually until the blown globe is found.

If twenty four volt twelve volt globes are used then there are ten lights. If twelve volt globes are used, then twenty lights are used, whilst if eight volt globes are used, then there will be thirty lights.

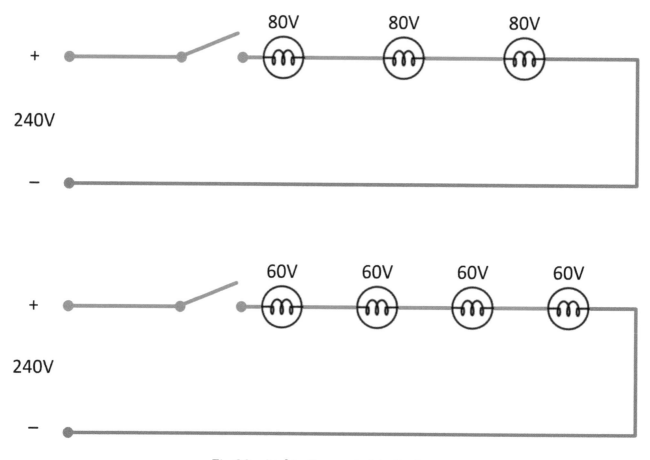

Fig 38 – Lights Connected in Series

BATTERIES

11.4   When Batteries are connected in Parallel, they maintain the same Voltage as one individual Battery. The more Batteries added the discharge will last a greater time than if one Battery was used. The more Batteries are added the longer the Output will last.

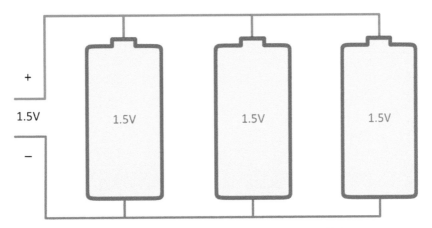

Fig 39 – Batteries Connected in Parallel

When Batteries are connected in Series, the Voltages are added together. Batteries are connected in Series until the desired Voltage is required.

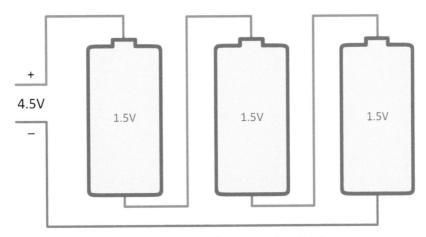

Fig 40 – Batteries Connected in Series

SUMMARY

11.5   Most appliances are connected in Parallel so as the same Voltage is applied to each appliance.

Series Circuits are not used very often, as the Voltage drops when it passes through each appliance.

When Batteries are connected in Parallel, they have the same Voltage Output as any one Battery, but their discharge time is extended.

Batteries are connected in Series when a desired Voltage is required.

Chapter Twelve

FUSES AND CIRCUIT BREAKERS

FUSES

12.1   If a fault develops in a Circuit, excess Current is drawn resulting in overheating. A fuse is the weakest part of a Circuit and will melt before damage occurs to the cable or Electrical components in the Circuit.

The Current drawn in a Simple Circuit is governed by the amount of resistance in the Circuit. If there is no resistance then a Short Circuit exists resulting in masses of Current being drawn and blowing a fuse or trips the Circuit Breaker.

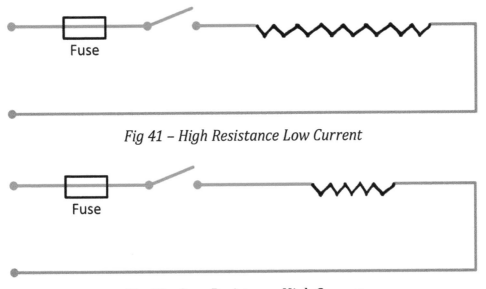

Fig 41 – High Resistance Low Current

Fig 42 – Low Resistance High Current

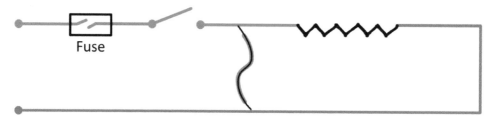

Fig 43 – No Resistance (Short Circuit) blowing a Fuse or Tripping a Circuit Breaker

A fault can exist in a circuit in the following manner.

In an A.C. Circuit a Short Circuit can occur between the Active and Neutral and a Short Circuit between Active and Earth, or a Short Circuit in a component.

In a D.C. Circuit a Short Circuit can occur between the Positive and Negative. A Short Circuit between Positive and Earth, or a Short Circuit in a component.

If one of the above faults occurs, it will blow the fuse. If there is no fuse in a Circuit then it would result in burning out the wiring or the component, possibly causing a major fire.

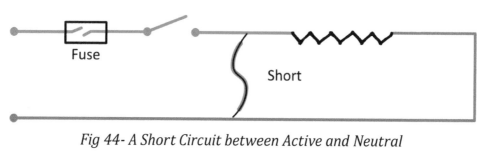

Fig 44- A Short Circuit between Active and Neutral

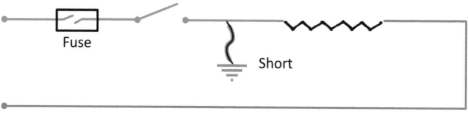

Fig 45 – A Short Circuit between Active and Earth

Fig 46 – A Short Circuit within an Appliance

Tinned Copper wire is preferred as fuse wire than normal Copper wire. If Copper wire is used as a fuse each time it is heated and cooled down, it oxidises. The Oxidising forms a flake on the wire which falls off and reduces the current rating of the fuse wire. Tinning the Copper wire prevents it from Oxidising.

Fuse wire is held in a fuse carrier. The fuse carrier has a base that is screwed to a fuse board or meter board and a fuse wedge which fits into the fuse base and holds the fuse wire.

Earlier type fuse carriers were made of Bakelite. Because of the high melting point of Copper wire (one thousand and nine hundred degrees,) the Bakelite became overheated and damaged.

Modern day fuse carriers are made from porcelain which can withstand the high temperature of melting Copper wire, but they have one disadvantage: *'Don't drop them'.*

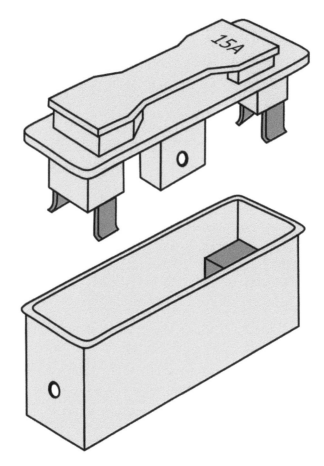

Fig 47 – Porcelain Fuse Base and Carrier and Wedge

Fuse Carriers are rated in Current and are made in different sizes to suit various Circuits.

Example: Standard Size Fuse Carriers And Fuse Wire For House Wiring

Lighting	10 amp Fuse Carriers	8 amp Fuse Wire
Power	15 amp Fuse Carriers	16 amp Fuse Wire
Hot Water	15 amp Fuse Carriers	16 amp Fuse Wire
Electric Stove	20 amp Fuse Carriers	20 amp Fuse Wire

It is extremely important not to replace a blown fuse with a larger fuse wire than the recommended size for that circuit.

The correct size fuse wire to use in a circuit may be determined as follows.

The fuse wire must be of such a size, that it would melt in one minute or less by a current equal to the maximum current carrying capacity of the smallest conductor in a circuit.

HIGH RUPTURING CAPACITY FUSES (HRC)

12.2   When fuses blow, they cause a mini-explosion. It is advisable that Circuits drawing Current in excess of twenty amps use High Rupturing Capacity Fuses (HRC). Fuses have the fuse wire encased in a cartridge and filled with Silica or Quartz Powder which quenches the Arc and prevents any explosion. They are commonly used in industry.

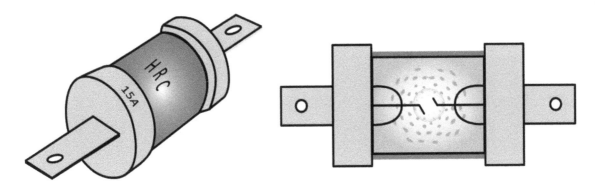

Fig 48 – High Rupturing Capacity Fuse (HRC)

CIRCUIT BREAKERS

12.3   Fuses may be replaced with a Circuit Breaker. A Circuit Breaker has the advantage, that as well as opening and closing a Circuit, it has the ability to automatically open under fault conditions.

The size of a Circuit Breaker is determined by its Current rating i.e.: 5 amps, 10 amps, 16 amps, 20 amps etc.

When a Circuit Breaker trips, the switch trips to the mid position, i.e. neither open nor closed. It can be reset by switching to the off position and then reclosing. It eliminates the problem of replacing the fuse wire, particularly with the incorrect size wire.

Remember a fuse or Circuit Breaker is a devise for protecting a Circuit from excessive current which could damage a Circuit or cause a fire. Never replaced a fuse wire with a larger fuse wire than, which is recommended.

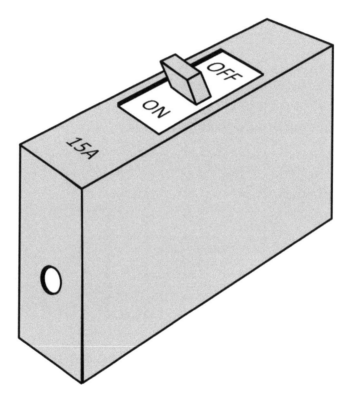

Fig 49 – Circuit Breaker

Chapter Thirteen

WHY EARTHING IS SO IMPORTANT

SAFETY

13.1   The most important wire in an A.C. Circuit is the 'EARTH WIRE'.

Any steel or metal container, containing Electrical wiring or Electrical equipment should be earthed. If the equipment is not earthed and an Active wire touches the steel or metal container it is deemed to be alive with Electricity. Any person touching the steel or metal container will receive an electric shock.

All earth wires are connected to the Neutral. When an Active wire touches any steel or metal container, a short circuit will occur and immediately blow the fuse or trip the Circuit Breaker thus, rendering the container safe.

As 240 volt A.C. which is used in our homes can result in a severe or fatal electrical shock. It is most important that all appliances housed in steel or metal containers must be earthed.

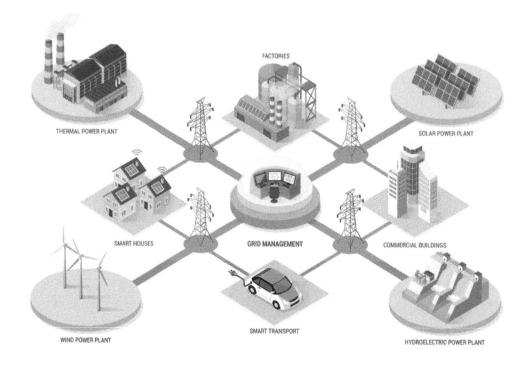

Fig 50 – Futuristic Smart Grid

Chapter Fourteen

LOOKING TO THE FUTURE

OVERVIEW

14.1 The last fifty years has seen a huge demand for Electricity, which has meant that Alternators have increased in number and size.

The tremendous increase in size of A.C. Alternators has meant a huge demand for fuel.

Alternators may be driven using many different methods:

STEAM DRIVEN
Most countries use steam to drive Alternators. Water is heated to produce steam, using coal or oil for fuel, and when burnt, have caused a major problem with global warming and pollution which is detrimental to the environment.

I feel sure, that if Scientists and Engineers had been able to look into the future, Alternators would be driven by a different method to what is used today.

HYDRO-ELECTRIC DRIVEN
Hydro-electric Power Stations use water to drive an Alternator, which is stored in huge dams above the Power Stations.

Some dams are built for irrigation purposes, so generated power is a secondary.

In America, because dams have been built, there has been a major decline in the number of salmon who travel back to their birthplace in the upper estuaries of rivers, to spawn.

DIESEL DRIVEN

Small towns and areas which are isolated from the National Grid System use diesel motors to drive Alternators. The diesel oil has to be transported at great expense and when it is used to drive the Diesel Motors it generates CO_2.

WIND DRIVEN

Over the last decade, small Alternators which are Wind driven are being installed in large numbers across the world, in areas where there is a vast amount of wind.

Wind operated Alternators are gaining in popularity around the world as they are very cheap to manufacture and install. They have no pollution but require consistent wind.

NUCLEAR POWER DRIVEN

Nuclear Power Stations are built in countries which have no coal for Coal-Powered Power Stations and is lacking in rain or snow for Hydro-powered stations. They are very cheap to run but have the disadvantage of nuclear fallout, which is extremely harmful to the environment.

Other areas which are being looked at to generate power, are the Ocean and Solar Power from the Sun.

OCEAN POWER DRIVEN

We have all probably stood in the surf and felt the strong force of the water on our legs and body; Alternators are being built harnessing Wave Power.

Scientists are looking to use the enormous power in the sea to generate power, which is also environmentally friendly.

In many areas of the world there are tremendous differences between high and low tides. Sea water is diverted into dams which are filled with the incoming tide. The incoming tide has enough energy to generate power and when the water is released with the outgoing tide, the power is generated again.

SOLAR POWER DRIVEN

The way to go!

Solar power has become very popular, as there is no pollution. This type of power is very cheap to manufacture as there are no moving parts, resulting in very little need for maintenance.

Solar power may be used in areas which are isolated from the grid system. It has opened up the possibility of building Caravan Parks and small country towns in many isolated areas that were deprived of electricity.

Solar cells are manufactured to generate power at different voltages of. 1.5 volt, 2.0 volt, 3.0 volt, 6.0 volt, 12.0 volt etc.

Many homes in the grid system use Solar Power enjoy the benefit of having free Electricity, whilst making a profit selling any excess power back to the supply authority.

Street lighting is also growing in popularity and was used in Sydney's Olympic Park for the year 2000 Olympic Games.

Satellites which remain in space for many years use Solar Power and many car companies are now building solar powered cars.

The way to go is with Solar Power. The only problem is that there must be sunshine. Excess power must be stored in batteries and used at night. D.C. in batteries can be inverted to A.C. for Household use.

Because of global warming from the use of coal and oil in Power Stations, alternate methods of generating Power must be found. Power from Solar Cells, Wind Power, Hydro and Ocean Power must be increased. Excess Power must be stored in huge Batteries for night-time use.

Many Countries in the world, like Australia, have lots of sunshine and should be using Solar Power.

Solar Power is the way of the future!

Chapter Fifteen

PRACTICAL ELECTRICAL EXERCISES

EXERCISE 1 – CREATE A SIMPLE CIRCUIT

15.1   The following Practical exercise may be carried out, by mounting the fittings on a piece of core board. All required components may be obtained at any Electrical Hardware Store.

USE ONLY Carbon Zinc Batteries.

Requirements:
- 1 Piece of Core or Ply Board (35cm x 20cm)
- 1 Four Cell Battery Holder
- 1 Miniature ES Lamp Holder
- 4 Size D Batteries
- 1 Miniature Electrical Switch
- Electrical Wire Red and Black
- 1 Six Volt Miniature Globe

Method: Install Apparatus onto the Core Board and Wire as per the following drawing:

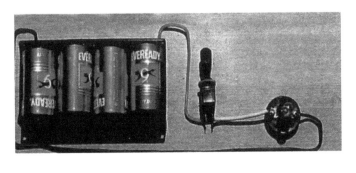

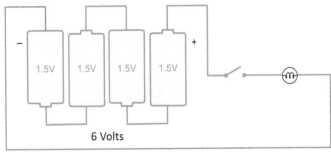

Figs 51-A and B – A Simple Circuit with Batteries Connected in Series to 6 Volts

CONCLUSION

A circuit is when an Applied Voltage A.C. or D.C. is applied to a switch and the switch is closed. The current will flow through light and return to the Negative, then the circuit is said to be complete.

EXERCISE 2 – 6 VOLT LIGHTS CONNECTED IN PARALLEL

15.2   The following Practical exercise may be carried out, by mounting the fittings on a piece of core board. All required components may be obtained at any Electrical Hardware Store.

USE ONLY Carbon Zinc Batteries.

Requirements:
- 1 Piece of Core or Ply Board (35cm x 20cm)
- 1 Four Cell Battery Holder
- 3 Miniature ES Lamp Holders
- 4 Size D Batteries
- 1 Miniature Electrical Switch
- Electrical Wire Red and Black
- 3 Six Volt Miniature Globes

Method: Install Apparatus onto the Core Board and Wire as per the following drawing:

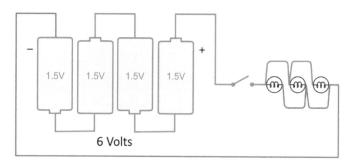

Figs 52-A and B – Three 6 Volt Lights Connected in Parallel

Note:
1. That all the lights have the same Voltage applied.
2. If one globe is removed, the other lights remain on.
3. Parallel Circuits are more common than Series Circuits because all the lights have the same Voltage applied.

CONCLUSION

Most Electrical apparatus is connected in Parallel as each appliance will have the same applied Voltage connected to it.

EXERCISE 3 – LIGHTS CONNECTED IN SERIES

15.3   The following Practical exercise may be carried out, by mounting the fittings on a piece of core board. All required components may be obtained at any Electrical Hardware Store.

USE ONLY Carbon Zinc Batteries.

Requirements:
- 1 Piece of Core or Ply Board (35cm x 20cm)
- 1 Four Cell Battery Holder
- 3 Miniature ES Lamp Holders
- 4 Size D Batteries
- 1 Miniature Electrical Switch
- Electrical Wire Red and Black
- 3 Six Volt Miniature Globes

Method: Install Apparatus onto the Core Board and Wire as per the following drawing:

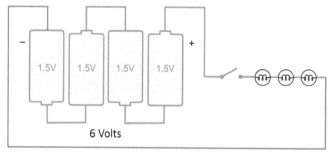

Figs 53-A and B – Three Lights in Series Connected to 6 Volts

Note:

1. That the applied Voltage 6 Volts are divided amongst the three globes i.e. 2.0 volts per globe. If four globes were used then each globe would have 1.5 volts per globe and therefore would be weaker.
2. The lights are not as bright as the lights connected in Parallel, because they have only 2.0 Volts on each globe as against 6.0 Volts in Parallel
3. If one globe is removed then all the lights go out, if a globe blows all the lights go out.
4. Series Circuits are not used as often as Parallel Circuits.
5. Switches are connected in Series with an apparatus.

CONCLUSION

Series Circuits are not used as often as Parallel Circuits.

Diagrams